ELEFRIENDS

STAR ELEPHANT JOKE BOOK

ELEFRIENDS STAR ELEPHANT JOKE BOOK

Illustrated by
Harry Venning

RED FOX

A Red Fox Book

Published by Random Century Children's Books
20 Vauxhall Bridge Road, London SW1V 2SA

A division of the Random Century Group
London Melbourne Sydney Auckland
Johannesburg and agencies throughout the world

First published by Red Fox 1991

Set in Century Schoolbook

Typeset by JH Graphics Ltd, Reading
Printed and bound in Great Britain by
Cox & Wyman Ltd, Reading, Berkshire

ISBN 0 09 983440 5

Foreword

In 1981 I stood on a hillside overlooking the vast plains of Kenya's Tsavo East National Park. The sea of thorny scrub met the washed out blue of the sky some twenty-five miles away and in amongst that carpet of greens and browns something 'red' caught my eye.

I raised my field glasses for a closer inspection and saw, with amazement, that the forest was alive — over 500 elephants caked in the Tsavo's famous 'red dust' were moving slowly away from the foothills towards the river.

It was a marvellous sight, that enormous herd. It must have been how early travellers in Africa used to see elephants when millions of them lived throughout the continent.

I remember wondering at the time, ten years ago, how much longer such herds would exist. How long before the poison arrow, the rifle and machine gun wiped them out? How long before they dwindled to a few scattered, terrified herds — some sad lonely captives at the local zoo?

But, while humans can be capable of causing destruction, carnage, suffering and devastation, so we can also show compassion, care, respect and understanding.

At the last moment, just when it looked as if the elephant might be heading for extinction, mankind said enough — the slaughter has to stop.

Now there are millions of people who care about elephants trying to reverse a decade of destruction. ELEFRIENDS, and everyone who cares about wildlife, are playing their part to 'save the elephant'. I don't think it's too late — not if we really want to help. Why not join them?

Will Travers
Director of Elefriends and Zoo Check

What is elefriends?

Elephants are funny animals — the world's largest land mammal but real 'gentle giants'. We make fun of them just as we make fun of someone we love but really the danger facing elephants is no joke.

Elephants are killed by poachers using machine guns and then chainsaws to cut out their ivory tusks. The ivory is used to make ornaments and jewellery. Not really very much to show for one big elephant, is it? Ivory looks better on elephants so people shouldn't buy or wear it. It isn't beautiful if it means we go on killing elephants.

During the 1980s the number of elephants in Africa fell by over half to just 600,000. Elephants were being killed at the rate of 2,000 a week — one every six minutes and it looked as if they might be extinct by the end of the century. But who could imagine a world without elephants? This is why ELEFRIENDS was formed in May 1989. We are the largest elephant protection group in the UK, supported by thousands of people, countless celebrities and nearly 200 Members of Parliament.

ELEFRIENDS helps the rangers in Africa's National Parks protect the elephants from the poachers by giving them the equipment they need — from simple supplies like boots and rucksacks to a mobile repair unit to fix broken-down Landrovers and a patrol boat to catch ivory-smugglers in Tanzania.

We all need to keep working hard to make sure the elephant has a safer future. There are lots of things you can do to help — from Jumbo sales to Trunkrocking discos. Just buying this book and having a laugh helps. If you would like to join Elefriends, turn to the back of this book where there is a joining form with full details.

Happy reading and remember not to forget the elephants!

ELEFRIENDS
Cherry Tree Cottage
Coldharbour, Dorking
Surrey RH5 6HA

A Message

When we asked you to send in your favourite
elephant jokes to the Elefriends competition
organized by Bookworm and Earlyworm, hundreds of
you responded. We're very grateful to everyone who
sent jokes in, for making us laugh and doing their bit
to save more elephants from harm.

Unfortunately, many of you sent in the same jokes.
We couldn't mention the names of all the people who
suggested the same joke or this book would be all
names and no jokes! So, where more than one person
sent us the same joke, we put their names in a hat
and drew out one person to be mentioned in the
acknowledgements as the sender of that joke.

Acknowledgements

The jokes in this book were sent in to Elefriends by
celebrities and the following children, who took part in the
Bookworm and Earlyworm Elefriends elephant joke
competitions. We'd like to thank all of them for taking
part:

Jemma Brannan, Ruth Marshman, Caroline Beaumont,
Kelly Reid, Ben Newman, Fiona Hancox, Paul Tansley,
James Essex, Michelle Walker, Meera Ruparelia, Emma

9

Khangaroot, Ravi Ruparelia, Ceri Louise Davies, Shelley Brown, Shawn Carpenter, Karen King, Carly J Farnell, Elizabeth Trairar, Aimee Hill, Terry Rust, Harley Day, David Robinson, Paul Summers, Paul Bowman, Lucy O'Reilly, Jason Sauvey, Deborah Keown, Kimberley Haines, Stephen Gilbey, Nimesh Gokani, Amandeep Dhillon, Manish Mistry, Tania Baldwin, Simon Bryers, Maris McKechnie and Emma Bryant, Christopher Dudley, Coralie Hurst, Amy Cheung, Stephen McIlwain, Alan Hughes, Zahreena Azam, Shabab from Broom Valley Junior School Rotherham, Asiea Bashir, Abigail Evans, Davina L Holker, Simon Webb, Francesca Szaniszlo, Kathryn Crooks, Laura Lamb, Tony Frizzell, Amy Sellers, Michael Dent, Edward Coppen, Robyn Brown, Carina Scheider, Louise Diggle, Sarah Revie, Paul Shaw, Helen Lewis, Michael Hooper, Richard Parrott, Sarah Seiles, Selma Ahmed, Paul Eastwood, Andrew Macdonald, Roisin Lightfoot, Stephen White, Robert O'Donaghue, Wayne Bell, Owen Pugh, Phillip Hutton, Michael Middleton, Arran McKee, Mandy McCleery, Martin Threafall, Rebecca Brett, Pamela Galbraith, Elinwyn Jones, Katherine Gawthrop, Eleanor Carleton, Aaron Foster, Lorraine Mills, Alexis Tizzard, Laura Elizabeth Kinsey, Cathryn Birch, Anthony Mercer, Katie Sykes, Laura Warren, Louise Newsham, Henry Heale, Carly Lawson, Alana Shilliday and all the pupils of the Abbey Primary School, the winning school in the Bookworm competition.

Special thanks also to Katie Wales, author of *The Elephant Joke Book* and *Return of the Elephant Joke Book* for her contributions.

Why don't elephants like penguins?
They can't get the wrappers off.

Stephen Fry

Where do you find elephants?
That depends on where you lost them.

What do you do when an elephant sneezes?
Get out of the way.

11

What's big, red and hides behind a bush?
An embarrassed elephant.

How do you tell an elephant from a grape?
A grape is purple.

What do you get if you cross a fish and two elephants?
Swimming trunks.

Two elephants fell over a cliff – Boom! Boom!

What do you get if you cross the M1 with an elephant?
Run over!

Timmy Mallett

When do elephants have sixteen feet?
When there are four of them.

Did you hear about the elephant who was
always drunk?
He kept seeing pink people.

Why do elephants wear green felt hats?
*So they can walk across billiard tables without
being seen.*

Gary Bond

What do you do when an elephant sits on your hanky?
Wait for him to get up.

What is the difference between a teddy bear and an elephant?
About 2,000 kilos.

What is the difference between an elephant and an orange?
Try squeezing an elephant.

What do you call the other half of an elephant?
The other half.

Why do elephants have trunks?
They'd look silly with suitcases, wouldn't they?

Michaela Strachan

What do you do if you find an elephant asleep in your bed?
Sleep somewhere else.

What do you get if you cross an elephant with a biscuit?
Crumbs.

Paddy Ashdown MP

What is grey, has big ears and goes ding-dong?
A belliphant.

What is grey, has big ears and is nice with ice cream?
A jellyphant.

What's the difference between a sleeping elephant and one that's awake?
With some elephants it's hard to tell.

How do you make an elephant sandwich?
First of all, get a very big loaf . . .

What has six legs, four ears and a trunk?
A man on an elephant.

What do you give a seasick elephant?
Plenty of room.

What has two arms, two wings, eight legs, two
tails, three heads and three bodies?
A man on an elephant holding a parrot.

What's got four ears, eight legs, two tails, four
eyes and two trunks?
An elephant with spare parts.

Why do elephants swim upside down?
So they don't tread on the fish.

What is grey, Italian and sings?
Tusker-nini.

Bill Travers

What do you do if your elephant breaks a toe?
Ring for a tow truck.

What is brown on the outside, grey on the inside and a meal in itself?
A wholemeal elephant sandwich.

What do you call an elephant in a phone box?
Stuck!

What's red outside, grey inside and very, very crowded?
A London bus full of elephants.

BECOME AN ELEFRIEND TODAY

What's blue and has big ears?
An elephant at the North Pole.

Felicity Kendal

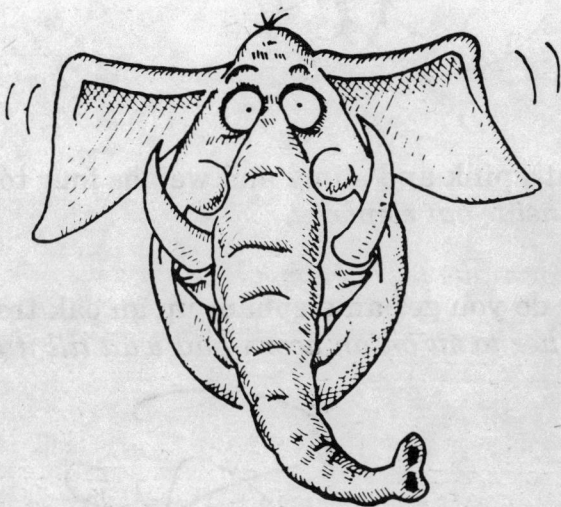

What do you get if an elephant sits on your car?
A flat battery.

What are two feet long, have thirty-two eyes and
two tongues?
An elephant's sneakers.

What's bright blue and weighs four tons?
An elephant holding its breath.

What's pink and slimy and weighs four tons?
An inside-out elephant.

How do you get an elephant up an oak tree?
Ask her to sit on an acorn and wait till it grows.

Sue Cook

Who lost a herd of elephants?
Big Bo Peep.

What did the elephant say when the crocodile
bit off his trunk?
'I thuppothe you think thad's fuddy . . .'

What did the river say when the elephant sat in it?
'Well I'll be dammed.'

How do you get an elephant upstairs?
In an ele-vator.

What's a hitch-hiking elephant called?
Stranded.

Why do elephants have big ears?
Because Noddy wouldn't pay the ransom.

Frankie Howerd

What do you call an elephant hitch-hiker?
A two-ton pick up.

What's the difference between an elephant and
an egg?
*If you don't know, I'm not trying one of your
omelettes.*

What do you call an elephant in rubber boots?
A wellyphant.

What do you call a metre-high elephant?
Trunkated!

What do Tom Cruise and an elephant have in common?
Nothing!

Owen Pugh
Runner-up, Bookworm Competition

Doctor, doctor, I think I'm an elephant.
Don't be silly, man, sit down and rest your trunk on my desk.

What's the difference between an elephant and a flea?
An elephant can have fleas but a flea can't have elephants.

What did the peanut say to the elephant?
Nothing, peanuts can't talk.

How do you raise a baby elephant?
With a crane.

What's grey, weighs four tons and flies?
An elephant in a helicopter.

What do you get if you cross an elephant with a hyena?
A big laugh.

What is the same size and shape as an elephant but weighs nothing?
An elephant's shadow.

What is the difference between an elephant and a mouse?
An elephant makes bigger holes in your skirting board.

Lysette Anthony

What's red, has a trunk and four legs?
An elephant with sunburn.

Why are elephants bad dancers?
Because they have two left feet.

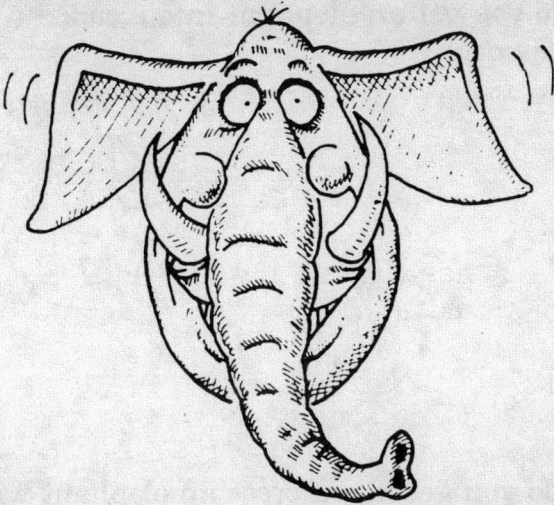

What's grey, weighs four tons and lives in California?
An L.A. Phant.

What's the difference between Gazza and an elephant?
An elephant can sing!

Wayne Bell
Runner Up, Bookworm Competition

What did Tarzan say when he saw the elephants coming?
'Hello, elephants!'
What did he say when he saw the elephants coming wearing sunglasses?
Nothing — he didn't recognize them.

Andrea Arnold

How do you get an elephant into a car?
Open the door.

What do you get if you cross an elephant with a computer?
A ten-ton know it all.

Why do elephants live in the jungle?
Because they are too big to fit in the house.

What do you do if there's a herd of elephants running towards you?
Jump in a telephone box, make a trunk call and ask for a reverse charge.

Michael Barrett

How do you make an elephant fly?
Push him off the top of a skyscraper.

Martin Threadfall
Winning Joke, Bookworm Competition

An elephant and a mouse went for a walk.
Accidentally, the elephant stepped on the mouse.
'Oh, sorry,' he said.

'Don't worry about it,' the mouse replied. 'I
could have done the same thing to you.'

How many legs has an elephant?
*Twelve — two in the front, two at the back, two on
the right, two on the left and one in each corner.*

How can you stop an elephant from smelling?
Tie a knot in its trunk.

Why has rhubarb got big leaves?
So you can't see the elephant nests.

How do you catch an elephant?
*By looking the wrong way down a telescope,
picking up the elephant with tweezers and
putting him in a matchbox.*

Why do elephants paint their trunks red and
their ears green?
*So they can hide in the rhubarb without being
spotted.*

What goes up slowly and comes down fast?
An elephant in a lift.

What do you get if you cross an elephant with a
hose?
A jumbo jet.

Sarah Greene

What do you give an excited elephant?
Trunkquillisers.

What's the difference between an elephant and a plate of peas?
An elephant won't roll off the end of your fork.

Tony Frizzell
Runner-up, Bookworm Competition

Why do all elephants have grey trunks?
They all belong to the same swimming club.

Gary Bond

Where does a 1000 ton elephant sleep?
Anywhere it likes.

What's the difference between an Indian and an African elephant?
About three thousand miles.

An elephant did a woopsey on the motorway.
The police say to use it as a roundabout.

What do you call an elephant that always cries
when it's hit?
A chicken.

What do you call an elephant listening in to a
conversation?
Big ears!

What do you get if you cross an elephant with a
potato field?
Mashed potatoes.

Ken Livingstone MP

What's big, grey and scary?
An elephantom.

What do you call an elephant with no teeth?
Gumbo.

What did the elephant rock star say into the microphone?
'Tusking, tusking, one, two, three.'

How do you get rid of a white elephant?
Put it in the jumbo sale.

What has feathers, can fly and can lift elephants?
A crane!

What do you call an elephant that flies?
A Dumbo jet.

What has four legs, is grey and jumps up and down?
An elephant on a trampoline.

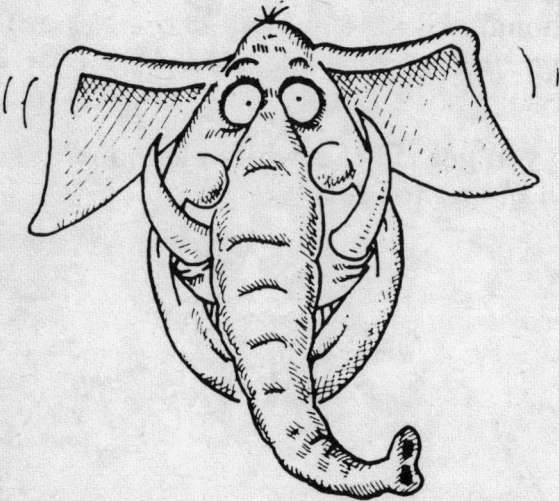

What can't you do if you put an elephant in your bed?
Get in!

How do elephants talk to their friends?
On ele-phones.

How do elephants get power?
With ele-tricity.

What do elephants watch in the evenings?
Ele-vision.

What do you get if you cross an elephant with a skunk?
A big stinker.

What do you call an elephant at the North Pole?
Lost!

What do you get if an elephant sits on your piano?
A flat note.

What do you get if an elephant sits on your best friend?
A *flat mate*.

Zahreena Azam
Runner-up, Bookworm Competition

What do you get if you cross an elephant with a budgie?
A *very messy cage*.

How can you tell if there's an elephant in bed
with you?
By the 'E' embroidered on its pyjamas.

Dawn French

Why does an elephant paint himself multi-
coloured?
So he can hide in a Smartie tube.

Where can you buy cheap ancient elephants?
At a mammoth sale.

When does a mouse weigh as much as an elephant?
When the scales are broken.

How do you make an elephant float?
Take a glass of coke, two scoops of ice-cream and add an elephant.

What is the difference between an elephant and a jar of peanut butter?
An elephant doesn't stick to the roof of your mouth.

What does the mother elephant say to the baby elephant when it misbehaves?
'Tusk, tusk.'

How did the elephant get out of the tree?
It used its trunk.

What do you call an elephant that can't do sums?
Dumbo.

What do you get if you cross an elephant and a germ?
Ele-phantitis.

Why did the elephant cry?
Because he tripped over an ant.

What happened to the elephant when he drank too much?
He got trunk.

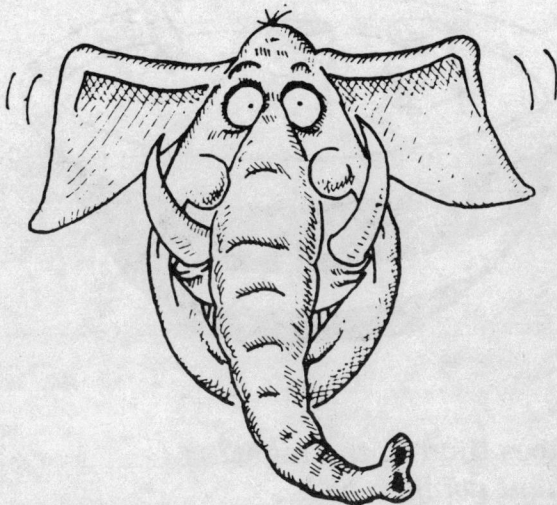

Knock, knock!
Who's there?
Hugo.
Hugo who?
Hugo and get that elephant off my garden!

CHEMIST: Yes sir, we can do life-size
  enlargements.
MAN: *Good, here's a picture of an elephant.*

What's yellow, weighs four tons and is covered
in lumps?
An elephant swimming in a bowl of custard.

What goes thud in the night?
A elephant going to bed.

Where do baby elephants come from?
Behind BIG gooseberry bushes.

James Rowley
Runner-up, Earlyworm Competition

What is the biggest ant in the world?
An eleph-ant.

Julie Christie.

Julie Christie and Henry Heale

Why does an elephant wash with his trunk?
Because he doesn't want to get his hands wet.

What happened to Ray when he was stepped on
by an elephant?
He became an X-Ray.

What time is it when an elephant sits on you?
Time to write your will.

What would you do if you found an elephant
eating your favourite book?
Take the words right out of its mouth.

What do you get if you cross an elephant with a rubber band?
An animal that never forgets snap decisions.

What do you get if you cross an elephant with a pigeon?
Dirty bus queues.

What do you get if you cross an elephant with a crow?
Lots of broken telegraph poles.

What's the noisiest thing in the world?
A elephant with a wooden leg dancing on a tin roof.

How can you tell that an elephant has sneezed?
His family's flown to the next jungle

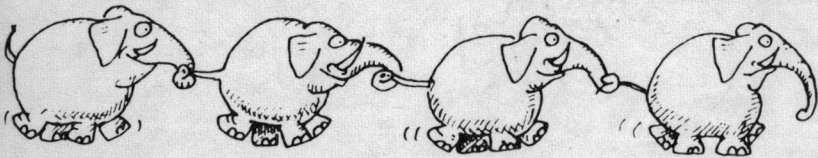

How can you tell when an elephant has cut its toenails?
The scissors are blunt.

What is the difference between an elephant and a banana?
An elephant wouldn't be pleased if you peeled his skin off.

What do you get if you cross a centipede and an elephant?
A walking earthquake!

What do you get when an elephant walks across a pavement?
Crazy paving.

How do you get an elephant in a matchbox?
Take the matches out.

What do you get if you cross an elephant with a rabbit?
I don't know, but there would be lots of them in a very short time.

Valerie Singleton

How many elephants can you get in a car?
Depends how big the car is.

What do you get if an elephant stands on your car?
Four sunroofs.

Paul Summers
Runner-up, Bookworm Competition

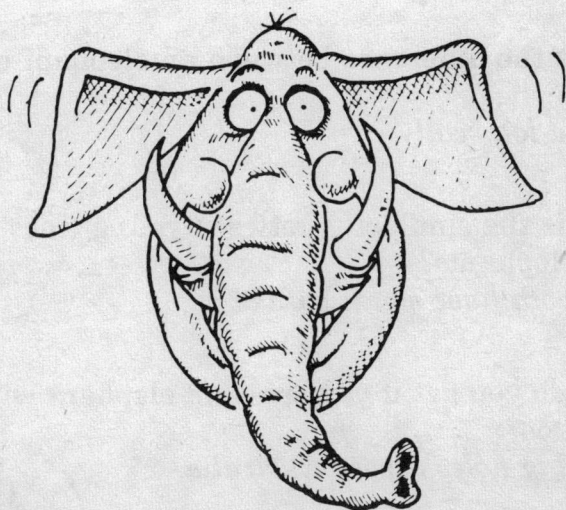

What roads do elephants take when they are driving?
Trunk roads, of course.

What's the difference between a toothbrush and an elephant?
You can't clean your teeth with an elephant.

What's the difference between an elephant and a flea?
Quite a lot, really.

What is the similarity between young trees and baby elephants?
They both have small trunks.

What do you get if you cross an elephant with a kangaroo?
Great big holes across Australia.

Penelope Keith

What do you call an elephant that never washes?
A *smelly-phant.*

What's got a long neck, is big and grey?
A giraffe disguised as an elephant.

What is green and has a trunk?
A seasick tourist.

What do elephants sing at Christmas?
Jungle bells.

BAH! HUMBUG!

Where do elephants get their TV licence?
At the elevision centre.

Which is stronger, an elephant or a snail?
A snail because it carries its house and an elephant only carries its trunk.

GIRL: What do you call a lot of elephants when they are all together?
BOY: *Herd of elephants.*
GIRL: Don't be silly, of course I've heard of elephants.

Laura Hunting
Winner, Earlyworm Competition.

PATIENT: Doctor, I keep seeing elephants with green spots.
DOCTOR: *Have you ever seen a psychiatrist?*
PATIENT: No, only elephants with green spots.

BOY: I can lift an elephant with one hand.
GIRL: *Maybe, but where would you find a one handed elephant?*

Pachyderms — a book by L. E. Phant.

Why do elephants paint the soles of their feet yellow?
So they can hide upside down in shark infested custard without being seen.

Sandra Dickinson and Peter Davison

TEACHER: Name nine animals from Africa.
PUPIL: *Er . . . a big family of elephants.*

What do you get if you cross an Axminster carpet with an elephant?
A great big pile in your sitting room.

Why did the elephant cross the road?
To get to the other side.

How do you call an elephant?
With a trumpet!

What do you get if you cross a jar of jam with an elephant?
A sandwich that doesn't forget.

Why do elephants have short tails?
So they won't get stuck in revolving doors.

What's big and grey and has sixteen wheels?
An elephant on roller skates

Why do elephants have wrinkles?
Well, have you ever tried ironing one?

Glenda Jackson

Glenda Jackson

What weighs 2,000 tons, wears a black leather jacket and goes 'he-e-ey'?
The elefonz.

What do you get if you cross an elephant with a flea?
Lots of worried dogs.

What do you get if you cross an elephant with a parrot?
Something that tells everything it remembers.

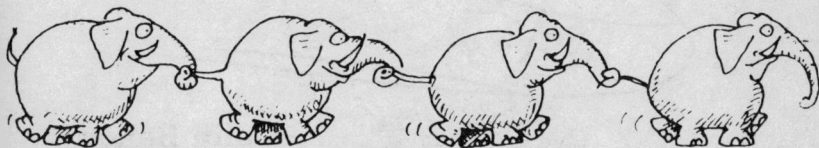

What do you get if an elephant playing a piano
falls down a mineshaft?
A flat minor.

Julian Lloyd Webber

What do you get if you cross an elephant with a
pig?
An oinkiphant.

What do you get when you cross an elephant
with a hibernating hedgehog?
A very heavy sleeper.

Which elephant won Wimbledon?
Jumbo Connors.

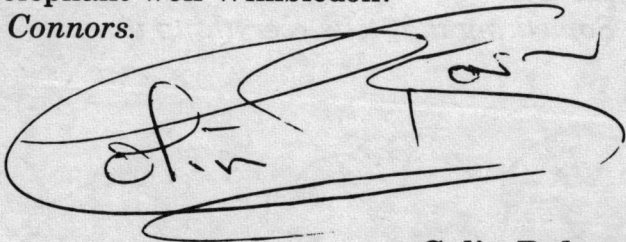

Colin Baker

What is grey, has big ears and writes for ten miles without stopping?
A ball-point elephant.

What is the difference between a gooseberry and an elephant?
A gooseberry is green.

What did Hannibal say when he saw the
elephants coming?
'Here come the gooseberries!' — he was colour-blind!

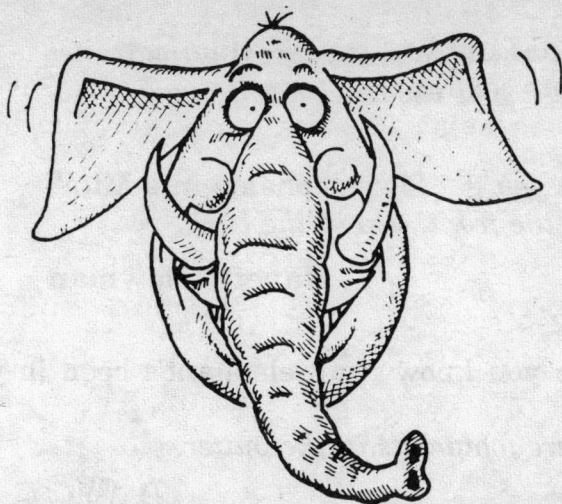

What is the difference between a gooseberry and an elephant?
Pick them up – an elephant is heavier.

What do elephants have that no other animal has?
Baby Elephants.

Katie Boyle

Who is Tarzan's favourite singer?
Harry Elephante.

How do you stop an elephant passing through the eye of a needle?
Tie a knot in its tail.

Why did the elephant cross the road?
Because it was the chicken's day off.

How do you get four elephants in a Mini?
Two in the front, two in the back.

Nanette Newman

How do you know if an elephant's been in your fridge?
There are footprints in the butter.

How do you know if two elephants have been in your fridge?
There are two sets of footprints in the butter.

How do you know if three elephants have been in your fridge?
There are three sets of footprints in the butter.

How do you know if four elephants have been in your fridge?
There's a little red Mini parked outside.

How do you run over an elephant?
Climb up its tail, dash to its head and slide down its trunk.

TEACHER: Can you tell me where elephants are found?
PUPIL: *They're so big, they're hardly ever lost.*

Why wasn't the elephant allowed on the aeroplane?
His trunk was too big to fit under the seat.

Hickory, dickory, dock, the elephant ran up the clock — the clock is now being repaired.

What has spots, weighs four tons and likes peanuts?
An elephant with measles.

What's grey, weighs four tons and goes 'Clump, clump, swish, swish'?
An elephant with slippers on its back feet.

What do you do when an elephant sits in front of you at a cinema?
Miss most of the film.

Virginia McKenna

What's white on the outside, grey in the middle and heavy on your stomach?
An elephant sandwich.

Why is an elephant big, grey and wrinkly?
Because if it was small, round and white it would be an aspirin.

Twiggy

What's the best thing to do when an elephant charges?
Pay and run.

What's grey, heavy and sings jazz?
Elephants Gerald.

What's grey, wrinkled and lights up?
An electric elephant.

What is the difference between an elephant's bottom and a post box?
If you don't know, I'm not getting you to post my letters.

SCHOOLBOY: I've got to write an essay on an elephant.
FRIEND: *Well, you'll need a ladder, won't you.*

What's grey, has four legs and a trunk?
A mouse going on holiday.

Esther Rantzen

What is grey, white, brown and has a trunk?
An elephant with his Sunday suit on.

What has a trumpet that blows every five minutes?
An elephant with a cold.

What do you get if you cross the ocean with an elephant?
Wet!

What kind of elephant lives at the North Pole?
A very confused one.

Why did the elephant paint himself purple?
Because he wanted to look like a plum.

Wendy Richards

An elephant always remembers but what kind of animal always forgets?
An owl, because it keeps saying 'Who? Who?'.

Where does an elephant go on holiday?
Tuscany.

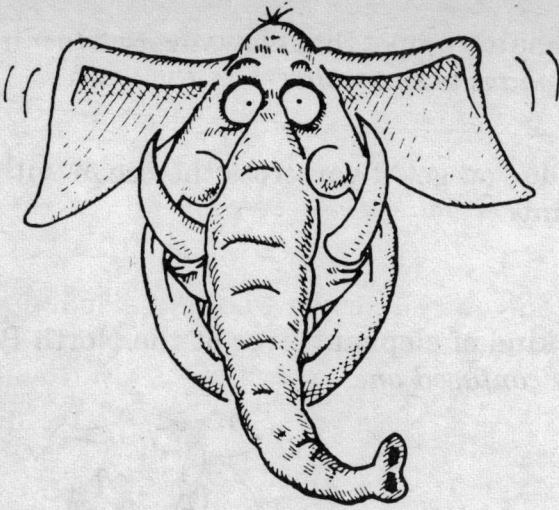

GIRAFFE: Where does your sister live?
ELEPHANT: *Alaska.*
GIRAFFE: Don't worry, I'll ask her myself.

What's big, grey and doesn't need ironing?
A drip-dry elephant.

Why do elephants have trunks?
Because they'd look silly with handbags.

What's worse than a porcupine on a rubber raft?
An elephant on water-skis.

CUSTOMER: Waiter, waiter, there's a fly in my soup!
WAITER: *I'm sorry sir, you'll have to leave. This is the Elefriends joke book.*

Why did the elephant wear red shoes?
Because his blue ones were in the wash.

What is worse than a giraffe with a sore neck?
An elephant with a nosebleed.

What do you call people who like elephants?
Elefans.

How many giraffes can you get in a Mini?
Two in the front, two in the back.
How many elephants can you get in a Mini?
None — it's full of giraffes.

Rula Lenska

What's the difference between an elephant and a potato?
You can't mash an elephant.

What's the difference between an elephant and a matterbaby?
What's a matterbaby?
Nothing, I feel fine.

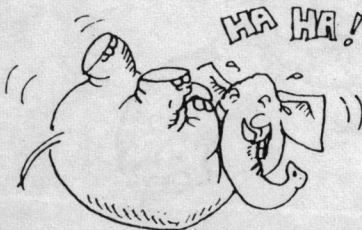

What is Nellie the Elephant's middle name?
The.

Joanna Lumley

What's grey, very heavy and wears glass slippers?
Cinderelephant.

When the biggest elephant in the world fell
down a well, how did it come out?
Wet.

What did the banana do when the elephant trod
on it?
The banana split.

What is big, grey and very dangerous?
An elephant with a machine gun.

DON'T PUSH ME!
DON'T PUSH ME!

Why do elephants paint their toenails red?
So they can hide in cherry trees.
Have you ever seen one?
No.
You see – it works!

Liza Goddard

What do you get if you cross a zebra with an elephant?
A traffic jam.

What do you get if you cross an elephant with a cactus?
The biggest porcupine in the world.

Why don't elephants have dandruff?
Have you ever seen an elephant with long hair?

What's big, wrinkled and green?
An unripe elephant.

How do wild animals greet each other?
'Hi Ena'; ''Ello Phant'.

How does an elephant overtake a tortoise?
He steps on it.

What did the grape say when the elephant trod
on it?
Nothing; he just let out a little wine.

Peter Duncan

Which elephants have the shortest legs?
The smallest ones.

Where do you find most elephants?
Between their heads and their legs.

If an African elephant fought an African tiger
who would win?
Neither - there's no such thing as an African tiger.

What side of an elephant has the most skin?
The outside.

What weighs four tons, is grey and loves curry?
An Indian elephant.

What do you call an elephant with a banana in
each ear?
Anything you like — he can't hear you.

Richard Briers

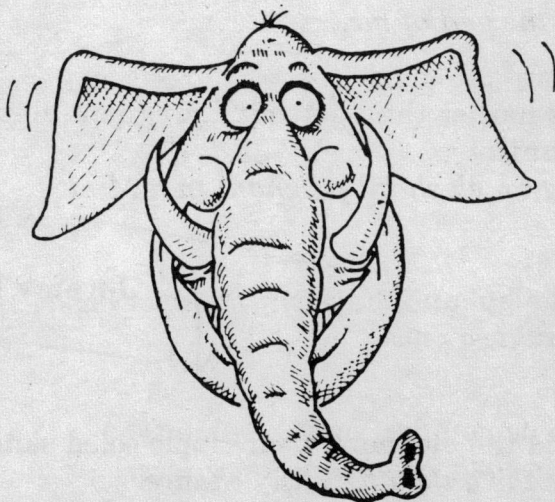

What weighs four tons, is grey and loves fish and chips?
An English elephant.

What goes in grey and comes out blue?
An elephant swimming on a cold day.

What looks like an elephant and flies?
A flying elephant.

What did the elephant say when the tiger grabbed its tail?
That's the end of me.

What's harder than getting a pregnant elephant in a Mini?
Getting an elephant pregnant in a Mini.

Jeremy Irons

Why did the elephant wear ripple-soled sandals?
To give the ants a fifty-fifty chance.

Why did the elephant paint his head yellow?
To see if blondes have more fun.

Why don't elephants play football?
They can't buy round boots.

Steven Fox
Runner-up, Earlyworm Competition

What do you get if you cross an elephant with a watchdog?
Very nervous postmen.

GRRRRRRRRR

Why shouldn't you go into the jungle at midday?
*Because that's when the elephants have their
parachute practice.*

Why are crocodiles flat?
Because they went into the jungle at Midday.

Deborah Keown
Runner-up, Earlyworm Competition

How can you tell when there's an elephant in
the custard?
By the lumps.

Bernard Cribbins

Why do elephants lie down?
They can't lie up.

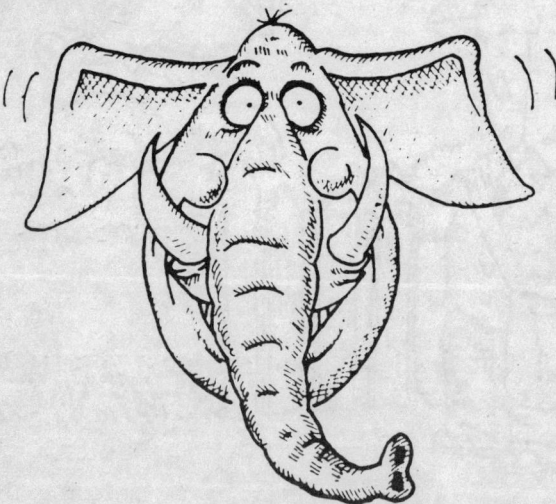

Is it difficult to bury an elephant?
Yes, it's a huge undertaking.

What is big and grey and bounces?
An elephant on a pogo stick.

What is big and grey, has a trunk and climbs trees?
An elephant — I lied about it climbing trees.

What is grey, has a trunk and jumps every three minutes?
An elephant with hiccups.

What is grey and powdery?
Instant elephant.

What is big and grey and lives in a Scottish lake?
Nessie the elephant.

What is big and grey and protects you from the rain?
An umbrellaphant.

What is the best way to catch an elephant?
Act like a nut and he'll follow you anywhere.

What is big and grey and plays squash?
An elephant in a cupboard

There once occurred a grand football match between the elephants and the insects.

The first half was a clean sweep, with the elephants scoring sixteen goals to the insects nil.

The second half was a different story, with the insects running rings round their lumbering opponents and banging the ball into the net until the score at the end of the match was elephants 16, insects 23.

In the showers afterwards, the elephant captain congratulated a young centipede who was the chief goal scorer for the insects.

'That really was a great performance,' said the elephant. 'I thought we had the game all sewn up. It's funny, but I don't remember seeing you in the first half. Were you playing in a different position?'

'No,' said the centipede. 'I was in the changing room getting my boots on.'

Hannah Gordon

And finally . . .

I have no elephant jokes. I regard the elephant
as a very serious animal. Indeed, it is its
sobriety of purpose that brings me to dislike
those who kill it to make its tusks into
chessmen.
   Perhaps, if it were told the rules, the elephant
would play better chess than Kasparov.

Donald Pleasance

Become an Elefriend

If you would like to become a FRIEND for a year and receive free copies of TRUNKLINE the ELEFRIENDS newsletter with details of merchandise, activities, and action to help save the elephant, then please complete the form opposite. Or you can become a JUNIOR FRIEND for a year and receive free copies of TRUMPET, the newsletter for young ELEFRIENDS with facts, figures, news, quizzes and special offers; or why not be an ELEFRIENDLY FAMILY or SCHOOL where you will receive both TRUMPET AND TRUNKLINE!

Yes, I would like to become a FRIEND for a year:

FRIEND   £12.50 ☐

Junior FRIEND (up to 11)   £6.00 ☐

ELEFRIENDLY School   £10.00 ☐

ELEFRIENDLY Family   £18.50 ☐

FRIEND (Senior Citizen/Unwaged)   £6.00 ☐

Yes, I would like to send a donation of:

£50.00 ☐   £25.00 ☐   £10.00 ☐   Other ☐

NAME _____

ADDRESS _____

_____

_____

POSTCODE _____ DAYTIME TEL NO _____

I enclose a cheque/postal order payable to ELEFRIENDS ☐

I enclose a credit card donation using the section below ☐

Credit Card ☐☐☐☐☐☐☐☐☐☐☐☐☐☐☐☐

Access ☐   Visa ☐   Card Expiry Date _____

Signature _____

Cardholder's Address if different from above

_____

_____

Please return this completed form to:

**ELEFRIENDS, Cherry Tree Cottage,
Coldharbour, Nr. Dorking, Surrey RH5 6HA**